The Great Big Rock
Learning to Surrender Every Detail to the Lord

Written by Tammy Schwartz
With illustrations by Eliza Morgan

Be Still Christian Publishing House

First Edition

ISBN-13: 978-0999399637
ISBN-10: 0999399632

*Dedicated to my faith-filled
counselor, friend, and sister in
Christ. You are a gift from God!*

CONTENTS

Introduction

Afterword

About the Author

INTRODUCTION

When my dad died, it felt like everything in my life changed. We lived together for years. We were best friends. We leaned on and took care of each other. When he was gone I felt lost. I began experiencing panic attacks. Things grew so dark and hopeless that I no longer felt the desire to keep going. I felt alone.

The truth is, I was never alone. My heavenly Father was with me every day. He still had plans for me on this earth. In order to encourage me and to pull me through my grief, He spoke clearly to me through signs, songs, messages, Bible verses, and books. He provided me with a dear sister and aunt, loving family, a supportive church family, and encouraging friends. He also led me into the office of an amazing Christian counselor.

She has walked with me through highs and lows. She has faithfully sought the Lord's guidance on my behalf. We pray and share Bible verses together regularly. It was my counselor's idea for me to expand on Romans 9:30-33. She knows how much I love to write and so she asked me to write a two-page paper on these verses relating them to my life.

Before I began, I asked the Lord to guide me in writing the words He had planned. *The Great Big Rock* was God's answer to my prayer. I hope that the words on these pages help you as much as they have helped me.

"What does all this mean? Even though the Gentiles were not trying to follow God's standards, they were made right with God. And it was by faith that this took place. But the people of Israel, who tried so hard to get right with God by keeping the law, never succeeded. Why not? Because they were trying to get right with God by keeping the law instead of by trusting in him. They stumbled over the great rock in their path. God warned them of this in the Scriptures when he said, 'I am placing a stone in Jerusalem that makes people stumble, a rock that makes them fall. But anyone who trusts in him will never be disgraced.[a]'"

Romans 9:30-33 *(NLT)*

[a]Isaiah 8:14 and 28:16

1
WILLOW

"Trust in the LORD forever, for the LORD, the
LORD Himself, is the Rock eternal."
Isaiah 26:4 (NIV)

There once was a girl named Willow. Her
Creator considered her to be a one-of-a-kind
masterpiece. He had great plans for her. He was
a wise and powerful Creator, but also gentle and
kind. When Willow thought of Him, she thought
of love.

She was excited that He had sent her on a
journey called "Life". Even though this journey
would have joys and sorrows and even though
she would not always see her Creator, she knew
in her heart that He would always be with her.
She would never be left alone. She believed that
He had the strength to help her with anything.

He gave her a Book of Instructions filled with
His words and told her that this Book would
direct her as she traveled.

The early part of her journey went well. The path was solid and easy to walk on. Willow lived in a house in a big forest with loving parents, an older sister, and four little dogs. Willow's family loved to take trips, visit museums and parks, go shopping, and spend time together.

Every Sunday they went to a special building where they sang love songs to the Creator. In that same building people read and talked about the words written in the Creator's Book of Instructions. The Book gave them directions on how to live. But much more than that, it taught them just how much the Creator loved each one of them. They learned that, with His help, they would reach the end of their earthly journeys and enjoy the Great Eternal Reward He had prepared for them.

****

When Willow was a teenager she faced the first great obstacle on her path. Her mom died following a long illness. Willow turned to the Creator for help. He was there for her. In fact, He carried her until she was able to walk again on her own.

As the years went on, Willow became more successful. She enjoyed keeping things organized and working hard. She was proud that people trusted her. Willow enjoyed helping others and felt encouraged when people liked her.

The Creator had given Willow a special job. She was to tell children all about Him. It was an important job, but it was a big job, too. Many days Willow was so busy, in fact, that she neglected to take time by herself to talk with her Creator or read from His Book of Instructions. Even though she loved what she was doing and felt blessed to work for the Creator, there were days when she felt slightly distant from Him.

As Willow grew up, the path on her journey was softer than it used to be. The pure faith she had as a child became clouded with a little pride, a few doubts, a growing number of fears, and a "to do" list that was far too long. Willow didn't know why the path had changed but she actually enjoyed walking on the softer ground.

Willow's family was changing, too. Her sister got married and adopted two beautiful girls. Willow's nieces held a very special place in her heart. Willow and her sister remained close and talked to each other just about every day. Willow and her dad also remained very close. In fact, they walked down their paths side by side for many years.

One of the biggest problems for Willow began the day she chose to carry a bag over her shoulder. Inside of the bag she placed all of the details in her life – good and bad. She would not let anything go. She wanted to hold on to every detail - forever! As she continued on her journey, she filled her bag with joys, accomplishments, fears, worries, and pain.

Willow felt secure knowing that all of these details were close by just in case she ever needed them. (She had lost sight of the fact that her Creator was also close by.)

The path at this point on Willow's journey was challenging. The softer path had given way to something that was much more like sand. The wind and the rain affected the path.

The wind caused the path to change directions unpredictably. She never knew where it would take her. The rain caused big holes in the sandy path that made it quite difficult to continue.

Somehow - each time Willow ran into an obstacle, she found a way to make it through by her own strength. She began to feel quite proud of herself.

That is until…

…the day her dad died.

When Willow lost her dad, her world turned upside down. They had been through a lot together. Her dad was her encourager, listener, repairman, and wise advisor.

The thought of walking down the path on her own was more than she could bear. Her bag of details had become too heavy already. There was no room to add the incredible grief she felt following her loss. It was just too heavy a burden for her to carry. But she tried.

She stumbled and fell again and again from the weight of her load. She was used to turning to her dad for help, but now he was gone. She missed their conversations more than anything in the world!

She also missed having someone she could trust with anything. Her dad knew her secrets. He also knew about all of the details she carried around. He had tried to encourage her to let them go. When she refused, he simply helped her to pack them neatly back into her bag. He thought he was helping.

As Willow continued to walk and stumble, she seriously considered stopping the journey altogether. She no longer had the desire to keep going. (Although she could not always see it, her Creator helped her through grief in many ways. He held her up and gave her strength to keep going even on the days she wanted to stop.)

2
THE GREAT BIG ROCK

One day when Willow was feeling completely exhausted, she decided to sit down and take a break. As she looked up ahead at the path, she noticed that something was different. There appeared to be an obstacle blocking her way. She wanted a better look so she got back up and walked a little closer. As she got closer, the enormity of the obstacle became obvious. She kept walking. It wasn't until she was about thirty feet away that she could clearly see that the obstacle blocking her path was a great big rock.

This rock was huge. It covered her path from side to side. There was no way she could get around it, under it, or over it. She said to herself, "What am I going to do? I've never seen such a big rock! I don't feel I have the strength, but I'm going to have to find a way to move it.

I need to keep going. I have worked so hard for so long and I have always found a way to make it through - even on the darkest days." (Willow did not realize that she made it through those darkest days only with the help of her

Creator. It was not by her own efforts.) "I *will* find a way to move this rock!" she said.

Now they say that timing is everything, and for Willow the rock could not have come at a better time. You see the rock that blocked her path gave her what she needed more than anything else in the world at that moment. The rock forced her to stop everything, lay down her bag of details, and rest.

3
DETAILS, DETAILS

Willow noticed even before grief had been added to her bag, that she could barely find the strength to keep going. She was *very* tired. She would learn soon enough that she was never meant to carry such a heavy load.

You might wonder what Willow had in her bag that made it so heavy. Let me share some of the details with you…

The lighter part of her load included awards she had won in school, pictures of the people she loved (and there were a lot of pictures because she loved many people), notebooks filled with ideas she had for her future and great memories she had from her past. These details were light. If they were all she had kept in her bag, she would have never gotten tired. Unfortunately, they accounted for just a small portion of the weight.

The greater portion - the much heavier part of Willow's load - included list after list of things she had yet to do. There were also worries about the safety of the people in her pictures. These worries made the pictures quite heavy to carry.

Next, she had a huge jar filled with all of the tears she had cried when her mom and dad died. She had also lost friends and pets she loved. Willow was afraid of being alone.

She also kept a book she called her Record of Wrongs. This Record contained pages and pages of things she wished she had never done and words she wished she had never spoken. She believed that she needed to work harder to make up for the things written in this book. Guilt was a heavy burden.

****

Worse yet, Willow wasn't the only one placing details in her bag. A dark snake that slithered around also placed doubts in her mind and one dangerous detail inside of her bag. The detail was a mirror, but it wasn't your average mirror. It was a two-sided mirror.

On one side, Willow could see herself. Next to her reflection, she could see a list of all of her flaws. Her weight, hair, big feet – they were all crystal clear inside of this evil mirror.

The other side of the mirror helped her to compare her reflection with the reflections of other people. What Willow did not know was that the deceitful snake had distorted the view so that she always saw the worst in herself and the best in others…

...Every time Willow looked in the mirror, she felt bad about herself – but she could not stop looking. It was another heavy burden to carry.

As if these burdens weren't enough, two of the details in her bag were heavier than all of the others combined. The first was a painful disease that Willow developed when she was just eleven years old. Not only did it cause her great pain, but it also took away her ability to have children. She kept this disease a secret because she did not think anyone would love her if they found out (only her family knew).

Willow talked to her Creator about her suffering, but never asked Him to take it away. After many years of struggling, a surgery finally took the disease away but left Willow feeling like she was not whole. Her body was better, but her heart was not.

The second of the heaviest details was one that Willow had carried for almost thirty years. It was an exhausting and overwhelming fear.

You may have heard that some people have a great fear of spiders, snakes, or flying in an airplane. Some people are even too afraid to leave their homes. Willow's great fear kept her from doing things that were routine and simple for other people.

You might think this kind of fear is strange or even funny, but it was anything but funny to Willow. At first, it was embarrassing but then it became a very heavy burden in her life. She did everything in her power to make sure no one found out about it. She made excuses and told lies. She missed out on trips and events. Willow hated this fear and even hated herself because she knew that the fear made her different from everyone else.

And so Willow and her details – light and very heavy - continued down the path on her journey until the day she came across the great big rock.

4
WILLOW'S BATTLE
AGAINST THE ROCK

Willow worried and even cried about this new and challenging obstacle. But then, as she always did, she decided it was time to stop feeling sorry for herself and figure out a plan.

Willow was determined to find a way to get by this great big rock on her own. She was glad to have her bag of details nearby. She just knew they would provide the help she needed.

She began by pulling all of her awards out of the bag. She laid them on the path next to the rock. Surely having such a great education would help her to calculate the best way to destroy this rock. She looked at the awards, but really, they were meaningless. They didn't talk to her or shout out any kind of solution. They just sat there on the path next to the rock right where she had placed them.

After a little while, she got so angry at the awards, she picked them up and threw them at the rock. The awards broke into pieces, but the rock remained steady and strong.

She wasn't about to let this rock win so she went back into her bag and pulled out her "to do" lists, her notebooks filled with dreams, and even her Record of Wrongs. She also pulled out the mirror of comparison given to her by the dark snake. She thought that she could use the mirror to reflect the sun's light and ignite all of the paper on fire. She hoped to start a fire so big and so hot that it would destroy the rock.

She did create a huge fire, but her plan did not work. All of her papers burned but the rock remained steady and strong.

She went back into her bag and this time, she lifted out the heavy jar of tears. She thought she might be able to pour out the tears on one side of the rock causing the sandy path to wash away.

By her calculations, when the sandy path washed away, the rock would roll off to one side and the path would be cleared.

It sounded like a wise plan but it did not work. As she poured the tears on to the path, they simply rolled under the rock. The sand absorbed her tears but the rock did not move. The rock remained steady and strong.

As she reached for her bag to come up with the next idea, she noticed just how light the bag had become. Many of the details she had been carrying around for so long had now been surrendered in her attempts to move this rock.

She couldn't help but acknowledge that if her bag had always been as light as it was at that point, she wouldn't be nearly as tired. "Enough of that kind of thinking," she told herself as she dug through her bag for the next detail.

Willow did not want to destroy the pictures of all of the people she loved, but she needed them in order to find a way to get around this rock.

Her plan this time was to stack up all of her pictures, one on top of another so that she could create a step. This step, she thought, might just get her high enough so that she could jump right over the top of the rock.

She began to grab handfuls of pictures. She stacked them one on top of another. But as fast as she stacked them, they sunk into the soft sand. She tried again and again until all of her pictures were gone. Once again, the rock remained steady and strong.

Willow did not know what to make of this. She was used to figuring things out. Now, in this battle she waged, she had not only given up almost all of the details in her life, but she was still unable to move this great big rock.

You might think that Willow was upset about losing all of these details from her bag. But she wasn't — not one little bit! Do you know why? Because for the first time in a very long time, she felt lighter and almost free. Thanks to this rock, many of the burdens she had been carrying around were now gone.

Willow finally realized that she would not be able to move the rock on her own. So she decided to do something she should have done many years earlier. Instead of turning to her own bag of details and trying to fix the problem by her own strength, she called to her Creator for help. She prayed with all of her heart.

The Creator made Himself known to her immediately (actually, He had been with her all along.) He was glad that she had finally thought to call on Him for help.

She had forgotten how kind, gentle, and loving He was. He patiently let her explain what was happening. He looked at her with great care as she talked to Him about all of the details and all of the effort she had put into removing the rock.

Finally, when she finished her long story, she stopped. It was time for the Creator to speak.

And this time, she was still.

5
THE CREATOR SPEAKS

Willow listened intently to what her Creator said to her as He spoke. Here are His Words...

"My Dear Child,

I love you. I want you to know that I have been with you every step of your journey. I know and I care about every detail in your life.

You have carried a heavy load that you were never meant to carry for far too long. You tried to keep control of everything, but the truth is, you never had control. The weight of your burdens became more than you could handle."

Willow agreed.

He continued, "I am the Creator of the heavens and the earth. I am strong enough. I am able. I am willing. I AM.

I was the One who placed this rock in your path to help you realize that you cannot make it through this journey on your own. The rock was meant to be a stumbling block that would lead you to see the simple truth that you need Me.

I love you and every one of my dear children so much and I knew that you couldn't make it on your own. That is why I sent my only Son, Jesus, to this world to be the Savior you so desperately need.

Jesus is the Great Rock in your life. He is not an obstacle to you. He is your solution. Jesus loves you so much that He gave everything He had for you, even His life. Through His shed blood, your sins are forgiven. You are washed clean! With His power and help, you can accomplish the great things I have planned for you. Jesus is the *only* Way to the Great Eternal Reward.

Let Me remind you of what it says in Ephesians 2:8-9...

'For it is by grace you have been saved through faith and this not from yourselves. It is the gift of God, not by works so that no one can boast.' (NIV)

The Truth is… Your works will never save you. You could never do enough on your own. My Son paid the price for you. The Great Eternal Reward is My gift to you simply because you are My child and I love you.

Jesus, My Son, is your friend and your Savior. His love for you will never change. He is powerful enough to help you with even the greatest challenges in your life. In your weakness, He is strong.

When your path in life changes like shifting sand, you can stand secure on Him. When winds blow trouble and sadness into your life, you can turn to Him for help. He is your firm foundation.

Jesus will take your dreams, your failures, your tears, your doubts, your shame, and even your sin. He is the Rock who will always love you and will carry your burdens for you. No matter what you turn over to Him, know that He will remain steady and strong.

As I said before, I am familiar with every detail in your life. I would like to talk to you about those details…

First of all, let's talk about the heavy jar you kept in your bag. You had filled it with your own tears. The truth is you did not need to hold on to them because I was with you every time you cried. Not only did I hear your cries of joy and of sorrow, but I also collected your tears.

David recognized this truth when he wrote these words in Psalm 56, 'You keep track of all my sorrows. You have collected all my tears in your bottle. You have recorded each one in your book.' Psalm 56:8-9 (NLT)

Willow - Give Me your tears, your joys, and your sadness. I will surround you with My loving arms.

You also carried in your bag many pictures and awards. Your greatest accomplishments and all of the people in your pictures were My gifts to you. Do you remember what it says in James 1:17? 'Every good and perfect gift is from above.' (NIV)

Your identity will never be found in awards or material possessions. They are great earthly accomplishments, but that is all they are. Your identity is found in Me. You are My dearly loved child.

And here is another truth…

You need not worry about the people you love because I care for them more than you could possibly imagine. Psalm 91:1-2 says, ' Those who live in the shelter of the Most High will find rest in the shadow of the Almighty. This I declare about the LORD: He alone is my refuge, my place of safety; he is my God, and I trust him.' (NLT) So trust Me to take care of the people you love in the same way I care for you.

I know you have lost some of the dearest people in your life. I understand your pain. I held you up in My strong arms when you couldn't stand on your own.

I know how much you miss your dad. He was another gift from Me to you. I know that you feel alone, but be assured that I am with you always. I will walk alongside you on your journey. Let Me fill the emptiness in your heart.

Let Me be the Father you turn to now for help and guidance. Talk to Me and give Me the opportunity to listen, encourage, and advise you.

Now - Let's talk about the book you have been carrying. It has been a heavy burden and has weighed your heart down with guilt. You called this book your Record of Wrongs. I am glad that it was destroyed in the fire you created.

Just as the book is now gone, so your sins are also gone. They have been erased, washed away by the blood of My Son, Jesus. Psalm 103:12 tells you that I have removed your sins as far as the east is from the west.

You can be free from the guilt you felt as you carried around that un-necessary book filled with your Record of Wrongs. Let it go. Give it to Me.

Next - Your notebooks full of dreams were wonderful. I love to hear My children dream about all of the possible ways I might bless them. But listen to this truth…

My Plans for you are greater than anything you could ever imagine!

In Jeremiah 29:11 it says, 'For I know the plans I have for you… plans to prosper you and not to harm you, plans to give you hope and a future.' (NIV)

Regarding your "to do" lists and your busyness, please remember two things…

When you are doing My Will, it will never be too much. And when you place Me first in your life, everything else will fall into place.

As it says in Matthew 6:33, 'Seek the Kingdom of God above all else, and live righteously, and he will give you everything you need.' (NLT)

Above all else, Willow, remember that nothing will ever take away My great love for you. Here is how Paul wrote about it…

'And I am convinced that nothing can ever separate us from God's love. Neither death nor life, neither angels nor demons, neither our fears for today nor our worries about tomorrow—not even the powers of hell can separate us from God's love. No power in the sky above or in the earth below—indeed, nothing in all creation will ever be able to separate us from the love of God that is revealed in Christ Jesus our Lord.'" Romans 8:38-39 (NLT)

The Creator continued to speak,

"Without knowing or understanding what you were doing, you handed over almost every detail of your life to the rock while you were trying to move it. What happened as a result?" He asked.

Willow answered, "My load became lighter."

"Exactly" He said smiling at her. "The words in 1 Peter 5:7 remind you that you can turn all of your worries and anxieties over to Me. I care for you and I want to carry your burdens for you.

In Matthew 11:28-30, I encourage all of My children to… 'Come to me, all you who are weary and burdened, and I will give you rest. Take my yoke upon you and learn from me, for I am gentle and humble in heart, and you will find rest for your souls. For my yoke is easy and my burden is light.' (NIV)

You no longer need to keep track of all those details. Give them to Me. Surrender everything to Me. I will help you."

Willow felt great peace in her heart. She thanked her Creator for the gift of His Words.

6
THE HEAVIEST BURDENS

The story does not end here, however, because if you were keeping track of all of Willow's details, you would remember that she had emptied the bag of all but two - the heaviest burdens – the painful disease and her great fear. (She also had not destroyed the mirror of comparison given to her by the dark snake. She simply used it to start the fire and then placed it in her back pocket for future use.)

Willow was aware that these details remained and of course, her Creator knew this too. He spoke to her again,

"My Dear Child,

Your journey will be so much easier if you will only choose to turn the last of your details over to Me. You do not need them. They serve no purpose in your life except to harm you and weigh you down. Trust Me."

"Could You please talk to me about them?" she asked. "Of course." He said.

"Let us begin with the mirror you have placed in your pocket. This mirror tells you lies. It has never given you a clear picture of who you are. You have allowed the mirror to convince you that you are not good enough, you are not talented enough, and even that the world would be better without you. This simply is not true.

Listen to how My Spirit inspired Paul to write My Truth in Ephesians 2:10, 'For we are God's masterpiece. He has created us anew in Christ Jesus, so we can do the good things he planned for us long ago.' (NLT)

I have planned and given purpose to each day of your life. You are special and you are needed. I knew you, loved you, and wrote about you in My Book before even the first day of your life began."

Willow knew as she heard these words, that her Creator spoke truth. She believed His Voice. She no longer wanted to listen to any other voices and so she pulled the mirror of comparison from her pocket and threw it on the ground smashing it into a million pieces.

Willow felt a tremendous release as if a thousand pound weight had been lifted off of her. She knew that the dark snake would no longer have control of her thoughts because her Creator was so much stronger!

"Well done." He said and then He continued...

"The next detail makes you feel as if you are no longer whole. You feel damaged by the effects of the disease you have had since you were a child. Your heart hurts because you were unable to have children of your own.

The pain from this disease was never My desire for you. It came to you as a consequence of living in an imperfect world filled with sin.

I am stronger than this disease. I work good through all circumstances. My Spirit has given you strength and love even in the midst of your suffering.

Listen to what Paul said in Romans 5:3-5, 'We can rejoice, too, when we run into problems and trials, for we know that they help us develop endurance. And endurance develops strength of character, and character strengthens our confident hope of salvation. And this hope will not lead to disappointment.

For we know how dearly God loves us, because he has given us the Holy Spirit to fill our hearts with his love.' (NLT)

Rejoice, my child, because I have made you whole. My Spirit has filled you with the love and the faith you need to carry out My Call for you. You may not have children of your own, but for many years now, I have used your life to touch the lives of countless children. You have faithfully taught them from My Book of Instructions. My Spirit has allowed the words you have spoken to fill the hearts and minds of these children with the Truth about life – eternal life – the Great Eternal Reward."

Willow thanked Him for this great blessing.

He continued,

"Do not compare yourself to others. Your journey is not their journey. Your comparisons have left you tired. They have wounded your heart. Remember - You are My masterpiece. You have everything you need to accomplish the plans I have for you. You do not need anything more."

When Willow was reminded that her Creator considered her to be a masterpiece and that He was using her in such a special way, her heart felt peace beyond understanding. She experienced healing from the brokenness she felt. One more detail had just been removed from her bag. There was now only one detail that remained. It was the largest and heaviest.

Willow spoke first this time, "My Creator, You know all things. You know that this last detail causes much fear in my heart. You know that I have kept it a secret for many years."

He responded,

> "Yes, I know. But I also know that it is time for you to stop hiding. It is time for you to know that you can trust Me with anything and everything including this, your greatest fear. I love you and I want to carry this burden for you."

With those words, the Creator's Spirit filled Willow with the courage she needed to go back into her bag of details one last time and pull out the final item.

When Willow held her great fear out in front of her Creator, an amazing thing happened...

It was no longer covered in the darkness of secrecy and lies. Instead, it was exposed to the Creator's great and loving Light. His Light dissolved the darkness that surrounded it. Her fear already looked smaller and more manageable.

"I am sorry for the things I have done to hide the truth from other people. I am sorry for the ways I have hurt myself and have even hated myself. I am sorry for the secrets I have kept and for the lies I have spoken." she said.

He answered,

> "I no longer want you to live in this way. It is not good or pleasing to Me. Always remember that you are a beautiful part of My creation. My Spirit lives inside of you as it says in 1 Corinthians 6:19-20, 'Do you not know that your bodies are temples of the Holy Spirit, who is in you, whom you have received from God? You are not your own; you were bought at a price. Therefore honor God with your bodies.' (NIV)
>
> I know that your sorrow over your sin is genuine. Therefore I want you to know that you are forgiven. You are free to walk this path, unburdened, hand in hand with Me."

Willow thanked the Creator for His forgiveness and then spoke again, "I must be honest with You for I know that You are aware of all that is inside of my heart and mind.

I confess to You that I am still afraid that people will laugh at me when they find out about my great fear. How could they possibly understand? I don't want to be different. I just want people to love me."

With great patience He answered her,

"You are right to say that I know your thoughts and words even before you think or speak them. I know all things. I know your deepest feelings and fears. It is good that you have chosen to tell me what is on your heart for your own peace and well-being.

The dark snake has deceived you into believing that you are alone in your fear and that no one will understand. You have been deceived long enough.

Listen as I continue to share My Truth with you…

You are not alone. I am your Creator. I understand you completely. I know your past. I know your heart.

I have walked with you every step of your journey and I have seen what you have experienced. I will continue to stand with you now and always.

There may be people who laugh, but that is only because they do not understand your fear. They do not know you like I know you. When you feel afraid, I want you to hold on to My never-ending, unconditional love. It will not go away.

I will also place people in your life who will understand. They will not laugh. They will seek to help you through this. They are My instruments.

I know how much you want others to love you. But seeking the approval of ALL people is pointless and yet another great burden you were never meant to carry.

Listen to the words of Psalm 118:8, 'It is better to take refuge in the LORD than to trust in man.' (NASB)

Finally, I want you to know that this great fear does not define you. You are so much more. I have given you not only unique talents, but also thoughts, words, love, and experiences that need to be shared.

As I have told you before, you were created for a very special purpose. No one else on this earth has been created to do the things that I have prepared for you.

You are unaware that many of My children share the same great fear and believe the same lies as you. They, too, walk around hiding the truth and feel great shame. They need help. I am calling on you now to not only believe the Truths I have spoken to you, but to share these Truths with as many people as possible. You, too, will be blessed and used as one of My chosen instruments."

Willow replied, "I have seen Your strength and power. I have felt Your gentle and kind heart toward me. I have experienced Your forgiveness. I am amazed by Your love. I am honored to be used as Your instrument.

I am ready to give this last detail over to You. I know that You are capable of removing this great fear from me and from many more of Your children if it is Your desire. I trust You completely. May Your will be done.

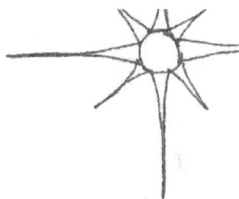

Tammy Schwartz   40

7
SURRENDER

At those words, Willow placed the last heavy detail into the hands of her Creator. He gladly accepted it.

She then dropped the empty bag on the ground and reached for His outstretched hand. She received strength and faith from His Spirit. She knew this strength would help her as she continued on her journey. Inside of her heart she felt a new energy and deep joy.

At once, with no effort at all, the Creator lifted her up on top of the rock. From the top she could see that her new path would be more solid than the sandy path she had walked for so long. Her new path was made from rock.

Willow looked forward to using the lessons her Creator taught her. She realized that she would face hardships on the journey ahead. She understood that being honest about her great fear would not be easy. She knew that the dark snake would continue to place temptations and doubts in her mind. But she also knew that her Creator was stronger than all of these things.

Willow took comfort in knowing that when the wind would blow and the rain would fall on her path ahead, they would not have the same affect on her as they had in the past. When she felt weak, her Creator would remain steady and strong.

So Willow and her Creator continued on her journey. Instead of carrying a bag of details with her, Willow now kept her Book of Instructions close by. When she was tempted to figure things out for herself, she remembered what the Book of Instructions told her, "Your word is a lamp to my feet and a light to my path." Psalm 119:105 (NASB)

Willow read from the Creator's Book of Instructions every day and talked to Him as she would a close friend, for that is what He had become to her. She felt lighter and free as she handed her burdens over to Him and let Him lead the way;

AFTERWORD:

Do you try to maintain control over every detail in your life? Do you face great fear or guilt? Have you lied to cover up secrets or sins? Do you worry? If so, then maybe you are as tired as Willow was.

There is wonderful news for you. Jesus, your Great Rock is just waiting for you to turn every detail over to Him. His love for you is unconditional. He loves you where you are at today and will help you to reach where He wants you to be tomorrow. Allow Him to lead the way. Give all the details to Him. Lighten your load and surrender your life to the Lord.

There is a reason God led you to the words in this story. I do not know the reason and I have not heard your story but I know that we all carry around burdens. My prayer for you is taken from Paul's words in the first chapter of Colossians,

"We ask God to give you complete knowledge of his will and to give you spiritual wisdom and understanding. Then the way you live will always honor and please the Lord, and your lives will produce every kind of good fruit. All the while, you will grow as you learn to know God better and better.

We also pray that you will be strengthened with all his glorious power so you will have all the endurance and patience you need. May you be filled with joy, always thanking the Father. He has enabled you to share in the inheritance that belongs to his people, who live in the light." Colossians 1:9b-12 (NLT)

Psalm 121 A song of ascents.

"I lift up my eyes to the mountains—
where does my help come from? My
help comes from the LORD, the Maker
of heaven and earth.
He will not let your foot slip— he
who watches over you will not
slumber; indeed, he who watches over
Israel will neither slumber nor sleep.
The LORD watches over you— the
LORD is your shade at your right hand;
the sun will not harm you by day, nor
the moon by night.
The LORD will keep you from all
harm— he will watch over your life; the
LORD will watch over your coming and
going both now and forevermore."
(NIV)

ABOUT THE AUTHOR

Tammy Schwartz has served in full-time ministry as a Director of Christian Education since 1993. Some of her favorite tasks as a DCE include co-directing Vacation Bible School, teaching youth Bible studies, working with puppet ministry teams, and overseeing youth music ministries. While this is the first book the Lord has led her to write, she regularly writes Bible study lessons, devotions, skits, and newsletter articles for her church. Tammy has a Bachelor of Arts Degree in Business from Concordia University – Wisconsin. She received her DCE Certification in 1993 after spending one year at Concordia University – Nebraska and serving a one year internship in St. Louis, Missouri.

Tammy currently lives in Central Wisconsin. In her free time, she loves to walk with her dog, Lilly, at local parks and to make quick trips to visit her family nearby.

****

;

The semi-colon at the end of this story is not a typographical error. It is a symbol that Willow's story is not over. God is still working out His plan in her life (and in yours) even at this very moment.

www.ingramcontent.com/pod-product-compliance
Lightning Source LLC
Chambersburg PA
CBHW060540030426
42337CB00021B/4357